WRIGLEY FIELD
HOME OF
CHICAGO CUBS

"It would be mind-boggling...There would be euphoria.
There would probably be a three- to five-month hangover."

– John McDonough, Cubs vice president, on winning the World Series*

*From *Wrigley Field: A Celebration of the Friendly Confines*, by Mark Jacob and Stephen Green

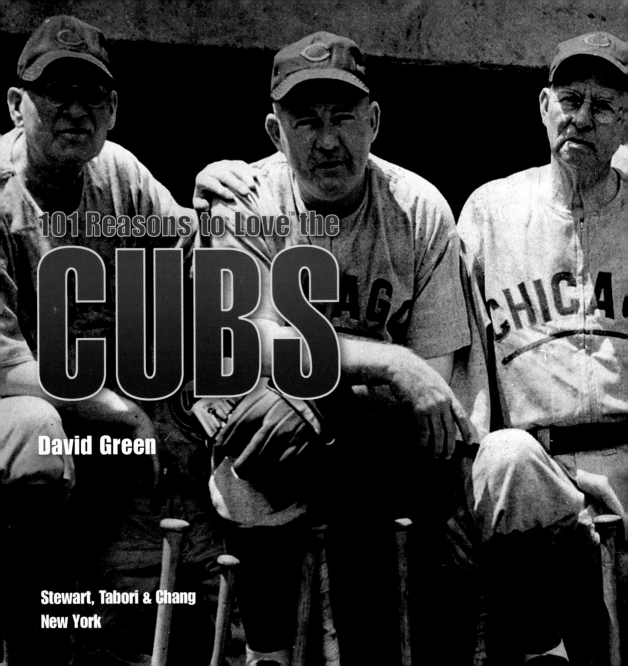

101 Reasons to Love the™ CUBS

David Green

Stewart, Tabori & Chang
New York

Introduction

Ernie Banks, "Mr. Cub," one of the game's all-time greats, spent 19 years in Chicago and never played in the postseason. Neither did Billy Williams. Nor Ron Santo.

Six decades have passed without a World Series appearance. Men have been born, grown up, played for the Cubs, and grown gray and wrinkled since the last one.

Six decades. But that's not the worst of it. It's been nearly a century since the Cubs won a World Series. A century! Wrigley Field is the second oldest ballpark in the major leagues, and the Cubs have never won a World Series there. For almost 90 years, fans have come to Wrigley full of hope, only to go home and see someone else win the World Series.

Forty managers—forty—have tried and failed to lead the team to the promised land since Frank Chance last did it in 1908. More than 1,500 players have taken the field in a Cubs uniform without winning it all. Heck, cars were just becoming commonplace the last time they won.

Put that way, it may not sound like it, but this is actually a love story. Why do you think all those millions keep coming? No team in baseball is more beloved by its fans than the Cubbies. Try telling their fans otherwise and, well, let's just say, be prepared.

That love has endured in success and, more often, in failure. Through thick or thin, it's there, that absolute devotion. Cubs fans personify the "wait 'til next year" philosophy so often recited in all corners of the sporting world. For nearly a century, that has been their mantra.

Theirs is a story that begins with hope, promise, and dreams fulfilled — but as the years pass, the story turns sad, even tragic. And, more often than they might wish, it has also turned humorous.

While hope has always been a part of every Cubs season, recent success has nourished and rejuvenated the franchise and the fans. In 2003, the Cubs were actually within five outs of returning to the World Series for the first time since 1945, before a historic collapse doomed them to further futility.

And yet they keep coming back for more. And so do the fans. It's a frustrating and often painful existence, but that makes the eventual reward all the sweeter. Someday, redemption will come and all of Chicago, along with fans everywhere, will pour forth in glorious celebration. It will happen. Believe it.

"Now, 0 for 50 would be a historic achievement on any other team, but on the Cubs it is usually called September."

—Bernie Lincicome

1 True Love

Isn't the phrase "for better or worse"? Cubs fans are as devoted to their team as any in sports, and they have to be to remain faithful. Lord knows, the Cubs have given their fans plenty of reasons to say goodbye. And yet, with the longest record of ongoing futility in sports history, failing to reach the World Series since 1945, and failing to win one since 1908, how can you not love the Cubs?

"What does a mama bear on the pill have in common with the World Series? No cubs."

—Harry Caray

Gabby Hartnett getting
a good luck kiss
from his mother

2 The Logo

It's a simple red C with white trim on the Cubs' royal blue caps. On the home jerseys, the word Cubs is spelled out, with the C embracing the smaller "ubs." And the blue "away" jerseys feature a blue bear cub surrounded by the big red C. No matter which design you prefer, the Cubs logo is instantly recognizable. Devoted fans display it proudly, not just in Chicago but throughout the country and around the world.

3 Home Sweet Home

No other major-league team has stayed in one place as long as the Chicago Cubs. Well, in one city, anyway. The original franchise, known as the White Stockings, was born in 1871, part of the National Association, but played most of its games on the road after the ballpark was destroyed in the Great Fire of 1871. The White Stockings went on to play at 23rd Street Grounds, Lakefront Park, West Side Park, and South Side Park, before settling into West Side Grounds from 1893 to 1915.

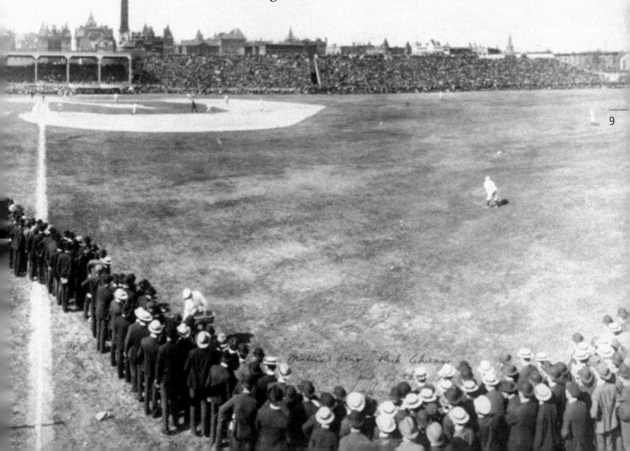

4 Old Glory

In 1876, fielding a team that featured former National Association stars Albert Spalding and Adrian "Cap" Anson, the upstart White Stockings captured their first pennant in the inaugural season of the National League of Professional Baseball Clubs, finishing six games in front of St. Louis and Hartford. Spalding led the league in wins with 47, and Ross Barnes hit .429, a club record that still stands today.

The White Stockings dominated the 1880s, winning five pennants in seven years from 1880 to 1886. Player-manager Cap Anson led a stellar club that included Mike "King" Kelly, Larry Corcoran, John Clarkson, George Gore, and Ned Williamson, who, in 1884, became the first National League player to hit three home runs in a game. During the championship run, Corcoran threw three no-hitters, in 1880, '82, and '84, and Clarkson added one of his own in 1885. In 1880, a remarkable 21-game win streak gave Chicago a 35–3 record on the way to a 67–17 finish, 15 games in front of second-place Providence. The White Stockings added pennants in '81, behind Anson's league-leading .399 batting average, and in '82, finishing the campaign by winning 17 of their last 18 games. In 1885, Clarkson posted an astonishing 53–16 record, along with his no-hitter, as Chicago won its fourth crown in six years. King Kelly's .388 average topped the league in 1886, and the White Stockings captured their fifth pennant in the remarkable seven-year stretch.

5 Anno Catuli

Loosely translated as "Cubs time," *anno catuli* denotes the amount of time, in years, that has passed since the last Cubs division title, National League pennant, and World Series championship. During the 2005 season, it read AC026097.

6 The Gloved One

The great Albert Spalding helped put together Chicago's entry in the fledgling National League and ran the team from 1882 to 1891. He pioneered the use of baseball gloves when he made the switch from pitcher to first base, in 1877, wearing a glove to help him catch infielders' throws and hard-hit balls. Before then, it was considered unmasculine to wear a glove, but, seeing Spalding wear one, other players quickly adopted the practice. Spalding, who was as good a businessman as he was a ballplayer, sold gloves in his sporting-goods store in Chicago, which over time became a sports-equipment empire.

7 Cap Anson

Adrian "Cap" Anson was Chicago's first baseball superstar, spending 22 seasons as a White Stockings player, the last 19 of which he also served as manager. In those 22 years, Anson hit over .300 19 times, including .399 in 1881. A very big man for his day, Cap wasn't afraid of anyone and often got into scuffles, sometimes with other players from his own team. An early advocate of the hit-and-run play, base stealing, and rotating pitchers, Anson led his teams to five titles in a seven-year stretch in the 1880s.

ADRIAN C. ANSON.
ALLEN & GINTER'S
RICHMOND. *Cigarettes.* VIRGINIA

Albert Spalding

Mike "King" Kelly

8 Mike "King" Kelly

The flamboyant, and extremely talented, King Kelly was one of the best players of his day. Cap Anson desperately wanted to add Kelly to his roster and went to California to get him. With Kelly in right field, Chicago won five National League pennants in the 1880s. Kelly was a great hitter who led the league in batting in 1884 and '86 with averages of .354 and .388, but his daring base running was what thrilled the fans. In the days of only one umpire, Kelly would wait until the ump had turned to follow a ball hit into the outfield; then he'd cut the corner in the infield, running directly from first to third, or from second to home. Despite his occasional disregard for the rules, Kelly was inducted into the Hall of Fame in 1945.

9 Great Names

Through the years, the Cubs roster has featured more than a few players with colorful names. Romantic names like Cupid Childs and Vincent Amor. Names that give food for thought, such as Sweetbreads Bailey, Ginger Beaumont, Pickles Dillhoefer, Peaches Graham, Peanuts Lowrey, Candy Maldonado, and Sugar Sweetland. If you're more of an animal person, there was Kitty Bransfield, Bug Holliday, Jiggs Parrott, and Hippo Vaughn. And don't forget such notables as Don and Howard Johnson, Jimmy Stewart, Mike Tyson, Doc Watson, Ethan Allen, and Trader Horne. There was even a guy named Al Heist, who stole six bases in two years with the Cubs.

"His strongest advantage was that he was always ready. He could take advantage of a misplay which others wouldn't see until afterward."

—Fred Pfeffer on Mike Kelly

10 Wild Bill Hutchison

Signed by Chicago in 1889, Hutchison won 181 games for the White Stockings in seven years. He led the league in wins for three consecutive years against the likes of Cy Young and Kid Gleason, winning 42 games in 1890 and 44 in '91. Hutchison holds the all-time club mark for complete games with 317 (in 339 starts), and he's second all-time in innings pitched with 3,021, third in wins with 181, and fifth in strikeouts with 1,224.

11 Colts, Orphans, and Cubs

During the 1890s, the press began referring to Chicago as the Colts. When Cap Anson was dismissed prior to the 1898 season, after a 27-year career and nearly 20 years as Chicago's skipper, the press took to calling the team the Orphans, which it adopted for a few years. The nickname "Remnants" became popular in 1901, when several players left to join the fledgling American League. After Albert Spalding sold his interest in the team to club president James A. Hart in 1902, Hart hired Frank Selee to rebuild and manage the club. The press then began referring to the young and inexperienced squad as the Cubs. The name stuck, and the National League franchise from Chicago has been known as the Cubs ever since.

Frank Selee, foreground, directing Cubs practice

"[Selee had a] flair for blending players acquired from here, there, and everywhere... a master at putting together a team better than the sum of its parts."

—David Nemec, *The Great 19th Century Encyclopedia of Major League Baseball*

12 Tinker to Evers to Chance

One of the greatest double-play combinations ever to play the game, Tinker to Evers to Chance came about through the genius of manager Frank Selee. A shrewd judge of talent, Selee convinced Frank Chance, who was riding the bench as a backup catcher, to play first base. He brought in Joe Tinker from the minor leagues to play shortstop; Tinker was a third baseman, but Selee thought he'd be better at short. Selee was right. And late in the 1902 season, after everyday second baseman Bobby Lowe was injured, Selee picked up Johnny Evers to fill the spot. Selee ignored the fact that Evers was a shortstop and put him at second. Thus, the incomparable double-play combination of Tinker to Evers to Chance was born. The three first played together on September 1, 1902, and turned their first double play the next day. Columnist and wit Franklin Pierce Adams, a New York Giants fan, immortalized the trio in 1910 in his poem "Baseball's Sad Lexicon."

They remained teammates until 1912, winning four pennants in five years from 1906 to 1910. The three were inducted into the Hall of Fame together in 1946.

These are the saddest of possible words:
"Tinker to Evers to Chance."
Trio of bear cubs, and fleeter than birds,
Tinker and Evers and Chance.
Ruthlessly pricking our gonfalon bubble,
Making a Giant hit into a double [play]—
Words that are heavy with nothing but trouble:
"Tinker to Evers to Chance."

"*Chance was a born fighter, a determined, able, and magnetic leader of men.*"

—The New York Times

Frank Chance

13 Frank Chance

"The Peerless Leader" was the anchor of the famed double-play combination of Tinker to Evers to Chance, and as player-manager, he led the Cubs to four pennants in five years, from 1906 to 1910, including a major-league-record 116 wins in 1906. Moved to first base from catcher by manager Frank Selee, Chance led the league in stolen bases in 1903, with a team record 67, and again in the record-setting year of 1906, with 57. He also led the league in runs scored in 1906, with 103. His .664 winning percentage as a manager is the best in Cubs history, and Chance's teams won 100 or more games in four of seven seasons. He was inducted into the Hall of Fame along with Joe Tinker and Johnny Evers in 1946.

14 Joe Tinker

Tinker was the man who got it started in the famed double-play combination. A gifted shortstop with exceptional speed, Tinker became a regular in his rookie year, 1902. Five times he led the league in fielding, and he stole 30 or more bases five times in 11 years with the Cubs. He even stole home twice in one game in 1910. Along with Johnny Evers and Frank Chance, Tinker entered the Hall of Fame in 1946.

Joe Tinker

15 Johnny Evers

Manager Frank Selee brought in the scrawny Evers to replace injured second baseman Bobby Lowe. Switched from shortstop by Selee, Evers became the pivot man in one of the best defensive units of the era with Joe Tinker, Frank Chance, and third baseman Harry Steinfeldt. In addition to his fame as part of Tinker to Evers to Chance, Evers was also the brains behind one of the most famous defensive plays ever made: "Merkle's Boner." He, Joe Tinker, and Frank Chance joined the Hall of Fame in 1946.

16 Merkle's Boner

On September 23, 1908, the Giants met the Cubs in New York in a late-season matchup that would likely determine the pennant winner. Al Bridwell came to bat for the Giants with two outs in the bottom of the ninth, men on first and third, and the game tied. Bridwell laced a hit up the middle. Thinking the Giants had won, Fred Merkle, who was on first, didn't run out the play, failing to tag second base. The Cubs' Johnny Evers recognized Merkle's gaffe — the rules state that any runs scored on an inning-ending force play do not count — and called for the ball. Confused, center fielder Solly Hofman threw the ball to third, where the Giants' Joe McGinnity, realizing what Evers was attempting, tossed the ball into the outfield. As fans rushed the field, Cubs third baseman Harry Steinfeldt grabbed the ball from a spectator and fired it to Evers, who tagged second base for the force-out. Umpire Hank O'Day, escorted through the growing throng of celebrating fans by Frank Chance, made the call, and declared the game a tie. When the season ended with the Giants and Cubs tied for first, the game was replayed in New York. The Cubs won the playoff 4–2 and went on to the World Series.

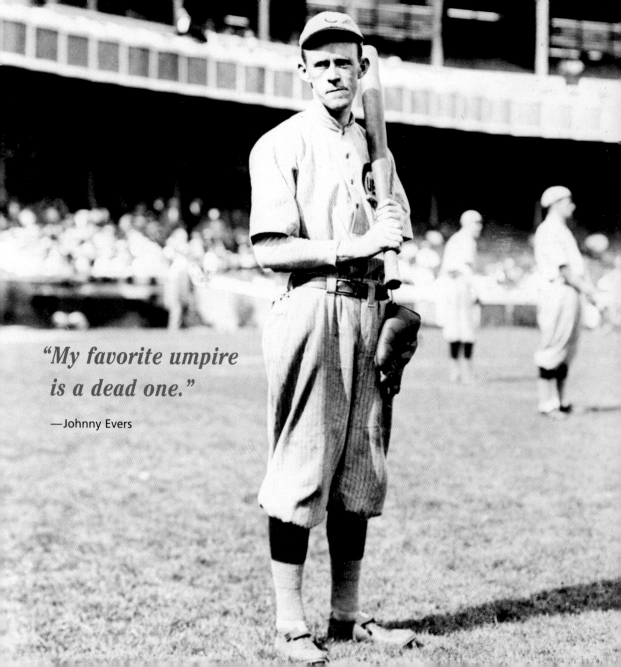

"My favorite umpire is a dead one."

—Johnny Evers

17 Orval Overall

Not only did Overall have one of the best names in baseball, but he was one of the best big-game pitchers ever, going 3–1 in World Series games for the Cubs. He threw nine shutouts in 1909, and his career earned run average of 1.91 is third all-time for the Cubs.

1906 Cubs: Orval Overall, top row, far right; Jack Taylor, middle row, second from left; 3-Finger Brown, top row, far left.

18 Old Iron Arm

Jack Taylor, known as "Old Iron Arm," set one of the most remarkable records in pitching when he completed 187 consecutive games that he started between 1901 and 1906. And if you go back to 1898, he completed all but two scheduled starts over the nine-year period, including 19-inning and 18-inning complete games. Traded to St. Louis in 1903 for 3-Finger Brown, Taylor returned to the Cubs in 1906, where his streak was finally broken when he left in the third inning of a game against Brooklyn.

19 The First and Last

The seeds sown by Frank Selee and tended by player-manager Frank Chance came to full flower in 1906. The Cubs overwhelmed the rest of the league with their dominant pitching, timely hitting, and nearly flawless fielding, as they posted an incredible 116–36 record. Their .763 winning percentage still stands as a modern-day record. However, despite 3-Finger Brown's four-hitter in Game 1 of the World Series, and a two-hitter in Game 4, the Cubs dropped the Series to the crosstown White Sox in six games in one of the biggest upsets in sports history.

In 1907, the Cubs' pitching continued to dominate the rest of the league, and this time it carried over into the World Series. After the first game ended in a 3–3 tie, the Cubs rolled to their first World Series crown, sweeping the next four games from Ty Cobb's Detroit Tigers by a combined score of 16–3. All four starters recorded complete games, and the 0.75 team ERA was a record that stood until 1950.

In 1908, the Cubs won a one-game playoff with the Giants, 4–2, as 3-Finger Brown, who replaced Jack Pfeister in the first inning, outdueled the great Christy Mathewson, sending the Cubs to their third consecutive World Series. Again the Cubs faced Ty Cobb's Tigers, and again dominated the Series. The Tigers put up little fight, winning only Game 3. Brown and Orval Overall finished off Detroit with a pair of shutouts in Games 4 and 5; each man notched two wins in the Series, giving the Cubs their second consecutive — and last — World Series title.

After taking a year off, Chicago won its fourth pennant in five years in 1910, but the Cubs lost the series in five games to the Philadelphia Athletics.

20 Mordecai "3-Finger" Brown

Nicknamed "3-Finger" because of a childhood farming accident that resulted in the amputation of the forefinger of his right hand, Brown came to the Cubs late in 1903 in a trade with the St. Louis Cardinals. Cubs manager Frank Chance convinced owner Jim Hart to trade Jack Taylor and Larry McLean for Brown, in what became one of the best deals the Cubs ever made. Brown won 188 games in Chicago, second all-time behind Charlie Root, including 20 or more wins in six consecutive seasons, leading the Cubs to four pennants in five years. He loved pitching in big games and won nine straight decisions against the great Christy Mathewson. Of his five victories in World Series starts, three were shutouts. Brown's 1.80 ERA in 10 seasons in Chicago is the best in Cubs history, and he also holds the Cubs' single-season record of 1.04, set in 1906. He was inducted into the Hall of Fame in 1949.

"...the most devastating pitch I've ever seen."

—Ty Cobb on 3-Finger Brown's screwball

21 Like Wildfire

Frank "Wildfire" Schulte is one of only two players in major-league history to record at least 20 doubles, triples, home runs, and stolen bases in a season. The other was Willie Mays. Wildfire's 1911 totals were 30, 21, 21, and 23, to go along with a batting average of .300 and 107 RBI. Four of Schulte's 21 homers were grand slams, a record that lasted until the Cubs' Ernie Banks hit five in 1955.

22 Charles Weeghman

Even though Chicago already had two major-league franchises, restaurateur Charles Weeghman brought a Federal League franchise to town and built a beautiful, state-of-the-art ballpark for his team in 1914. After a couple of years, the Federal League folded, but Weeghman, who ran a very successful Chicago franchise, was given the opportunity to purchase a controlling interest in the Cubs. Joe Tinker, then the player-manager of the Federal League's Whalers, was brought back to manage the Cubs as Weeghman merged the two teams. With the merger came the beautiful Weeghman Park, which would eventually become known as Wrigley Field. Weeghman's Cubs made it to the World Series in 1918, losing to the Red Sox in six games, but in 1919, suffering financially, Weeghman sold the team to William Wrigley Jr.

Charles Weeghman, center in straw hat, and Joe Tinker, in plaid cap, with members of the Wide Awake Club

23 The Friendly Confines

It's a magical place. A place where hope lives—and too often dies. A place where generation after generation has come to spend a day at the park and cheer on their beloved Cubs. A timeless place, much the same since the late 1930s when the center-field scoreboard, the ivy-covered outfield walls, and the bleachers just beyond, which play host to the lovable "Bleacher Bums," were added.

Originally built by Charles Weeghman, owner of the Federal League Chicago Whalers, in 1914, on a site that was once a picnic area and later a seminary, the concrete-and-steel structure is the second-oldest ballpark still in use in the major leagues. Only Boston's Fenway Park, built in 1912, is older.

After the Federal League folded in 1915, Weeghman bought the Cubs from Charles Taft and moved the team into his beautiful ballpark. William Wrigley Jr. eventually took over the team, and in 1926 the ballpark was renamed Wrigley Field. Over time it has become known as "the friendly confines." It may be the perfect description.

24 The Rooftops

Beyond the ivy-covered outfield fences and the denizen-filled bleachers of Wrigley Field are the rooftops of the buildings that flank Waveland and Sheffield avenues. From the tops of these buildings, fans can get a distant glimpse of the action in Wrigley while enjoying their own private parties. What was once a quaint pastime has now grown into a small cottage industry, where admission to catered events can cost upwards of $100. Many of the rooftops now feature their own bleachers, allowing more fans to share in the excitement.

25 Ballhawks

There's a whole 'nother game out on Waveland Avenue while the Cubs play inside Wrigley Field. Ballhawks, some gloved, others barehanded, stand at the ready for any and every ball hit out of the park and onto the avenue. The resulting scrum can get physical, and the 'hawks risk bumps, scrapes, bruises, and sometimes worse to grab the special souvenir. A few guys have made something of a career out of it, spending years, even decades, on the street chasing balls. Gary "Moe" Mullins, one of the all-time greats, is said to have snagged well over 3,000 balls in his "career." Considering there are 81 home games each season, he would have to average 2 balls per game for nearly 20 years to reach that total. Go figure.

26 No Means No

Way back on May 2, 1917, the Cubs' Hippo Vaughn and the Reds' Fred Toney staged one of the greatest pitchers' duels ever, each throwing a no-hitter for nine innings. Sadly, the game had to come to an end somehow. Even sadder, it was the Cubs' Vaughn who faltered first. Vaughn gave up a sharp single to Larry Kopf in the top of the 10th. After Hal Chase reached on an error, Jim Thorpe, of Olympic fame, chopped one out in front of the plate that Vaughn fielded and fired to catcher Art Wilson. But Wilson, not expecting the throw, bobbled the ball and Kopf scored. When Toney finished off the Cubs in the bottom of the tenth, preserving his no-hitter, the Reds had won, 1–0. Vaughn went on to be the greatest left-hander in Cubs history, winning 20 or more games five times.

27 The White Sox

Cubs fans will tell you that no "true" Chicagoan watches baseball down in south Chicago. Even when the White Sox are in the thick of things, the Cubs routinely outdraw the Sox. Cubs fans will also remind you that their team never cheated, never threw a World Series. Hmm. Guess the friendly confines don't extend to Chicago's south side.

"Big Jim Vaughn used to pitch the particular kind of ball a batter liked best just to show him that he couldn't hit it. Nothing pleased him better than to strike a man out pitching to his strength."

—Grover Cleveland Alexander

The 1918 starting rotation: Lefty Tyler, Hippo Vaughn, Phil Douglas, and Claude Hendrix

28 William Wrigley Jr.

When Charles Weeghman was forced to sell the Cubs in 1919, William Wrigley Jr., who had a small stake in the team, stepped in and bought it — the start of over 60 years of ownership by the Wrigley family. Wrigley, the son of a soap maker, had come to Chicago from Philadelphia, starting his own business selling Wrigley's Scouring Soap. That led to selling baking soda, and the baking soda led to chewing gum. Wrigley made millions in the chewing-gum business, and he brought his salesmanship and innovative thinking to the Cubs.

He hired William Veeck Sr. to run the baseball club, and together the two introduced many new ideas to the game. In 1925, they pioneered the radio broadcast of games, and later they initiated "Ladies Day," which provided free tickets to women for games played on Fridays. Anticipating that many of these women would bring their children along, the Wrigleys successfully nurtured another generation of fans with this simple, friendly promotion. The idea was so popular during the 1930s that tickets had to be requested by mail.

Wrigley was revered by his players and loved by fans, who flooded through the ballpark's gates in record numbers. To honor Wrigley, Cubs Park was renamed Wrigley Field in 1926. Unfortunately, the Cubs made it to only one World Series under Wrigley's stewardship, losing to the Philadelphia Athletics in 1929. Wrigley died in 1932, and his son Philip took over the team.

"Wrigley was a heck of a salesman, a great owner, and a fair man."

—Derek Gentile, *The Complete Chicago Cubs*

29 Catalina Island

It has to be the best spring-training location in the history of baseball. From 1921 through 1951, William Wrigley had his Cubs team prepare for the upcoming season on the spectacular Catalina Island, off the coast of Southern California. When practice was over, Wrigley provided plenty of diversions for his players, including barbecues at his mountaintop mansion, fishing trips, and even mountain-goat rodeos. Although the players didn't necessarily enjoy the vigorous hikes up the mountains, they fell in love with the place. Even the ever-ornery Rogers Hornsby seemed to like it there.

30 West Coast Wrigley

In what is now South Central Los Angeles, Wrigley built a mini–Wrigley Field, which hosted Pacific Coast League games for years and was used as the baseball setting for numerous movies, including *Pride of the Yankees*, *The Pride of St. Louis*, and *The Winning Team* (featuring Ronald Reagan as Grover Cleveland Alexander). The Dodgers thought about making the other Wrigley their home when they abruptly left Brooklyn, and the California Angels did play their first season at the 20,000-seat stadium, in 1961.

31 Four in 10

Following their great run from 1906 to 1910, the Cubs won only one pennant, in 1918, until 1929. The infamous 1918 season ended with a loss to the Red Sox in the World Series — the last time either team would win the Series until 2004, when the Sox finally broke their curse.

The Cubs' 1929 pennant started a run of four in 10 years. Future Hall of Famer Rogers Hornsby led the way in '29, hitting .380 with 39 homers and 149 RBI. But the Cubs dropped the Series to the Philadelphia Athletics in five games.

In 1932, Hornsby was fired after a year and a half as manager and first baseman Charlie Grimm took over. The Cubs won the pennant, but they were swept by the New York Yankees in the World Series that featured Babe Ruth's "Called Shot."

CHICAGO "CUBS" NATIONAL LEAGUE P

The 1935 season saw the Cubs win another pennant, as they roared back from a 9 1/2-game deficit at the All-Star break and won an amazing 21 games in a row as the regular season wound down. Billy Herman and Augie Galan were key contributors during the streak. But the Cubs couldn't maintain their momentum and again they lost the World Series, this time to the Detroit Tigers in six games.

Three years later, Chicago put together another incredible late-season streak, at one point winning 20 of 24 games. Gabby Hartnett's "Homer in the Gloamin'" won a key late-season contest against the Pittsburgh Pirates, but the Yankees juggernaut swept the Cubs in the World Series. In the 10-year period, the Cubs had won four pennants, along with three second-place and three third-place finishes.

NT WINNERS 1929

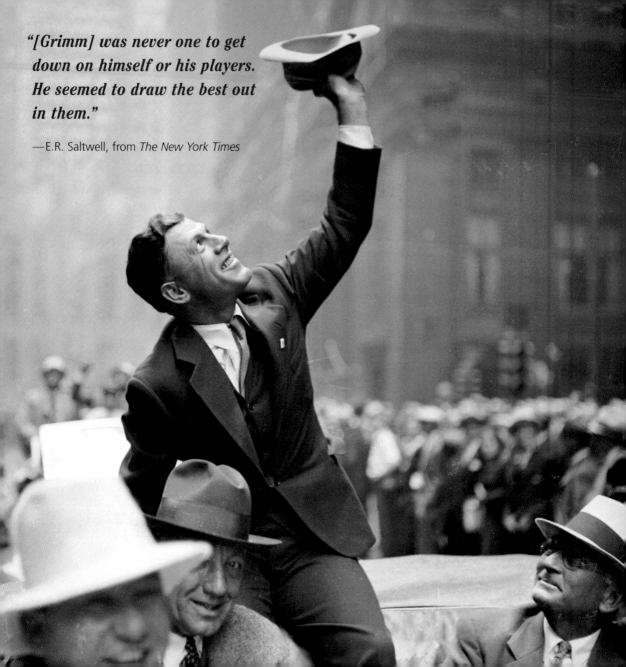

"*[Grimm] was never one to get down on himself or his players. He seemed to draw the best out in them.*"

—E.R. Saltwell, from *The New York Times*

32 Rogers Hornsby

Believed to be past his prime when he was traded to the Cubs in 1929, Hornsby went out and proved his critics wrong by hitting .380 and leading the league in runs scored. Playing every inning of every game, he won the league's Most Valuable Player award and helped the Cubs win the pennant that year. He was named manager in 1930 and, in 1931, became the first major leaguer to hit an extra-inning grand slam. The brusque Hornsby's stint as manager was cut short in 1932, when he was replaced by the jovial Charlie Grimm, but Hornsby continued to play until 1937, returning to St. Louis to finish his career. Hornsby was inducted into the Hall of Fame in 1942.

33 Charlie Grimm

"Jolly Cholly" came to Chicago with Rabbit Maranville in a trade with Pittsburgh in 1925. Grimm, an excellent defensive first baseman, hit .306 in his first year in Chicago and .296 during his 12 years with the Cubs. In 1932, when the stern Rogers Hornsby was let go as manager, the fun-loving, banjo-playing Grimm stepped in to lead the Cubs to the National League pennant. In 1935, Jolly Cholly took the Cubs back to the World Series, but by 1938, feeling like he was out of touch with his players, he resigned in mid-season. Grimm moved to the broadcast booth, but in 1945 he returned to the dugout and led the Cubs to their final pennant. Let go in 1949, Grimm returned for a third and final stint in 1960, but he resigned after just 17 games. In a unique trade, Grimm went back to the broadcast booth, and broadcaster Lou Boudreau took over the managerial reins. Only in Chicago!

"He's the only guy I know who could hit .350 in the dark."

—Frankie Frisch on Rogers Hornsby

34 The Incredibles

The 1929 Cubs outfield of Hack Wilson, Riggs Stephenson, and Kiki Cuyler is the only group in National League history to drive in more than 100 runs each in the same season. Wilson led the way with 159 RBI. Stephenson added 110, and Cuyler chipped in 102. They batted .345, .362, and .360, respectively.

35 Kiki Cuyler

Acquired in a trade with Pittsburgh, Cuyler teamed with Riggs Stephenson and Hack Wilson to form one of the most potent outfields of all time. In 1929, the trio collectively hit .350, with 71 home runs and 371 RBI. Cuyler hit over .300 five times with the Cubs, including .360 in 1929 and .355 in 1930, and led the National League in stolen bases three straight years, from 1928 to 1930 (37, 43, 37). He was inducted into the Hall of Fame in 1968.

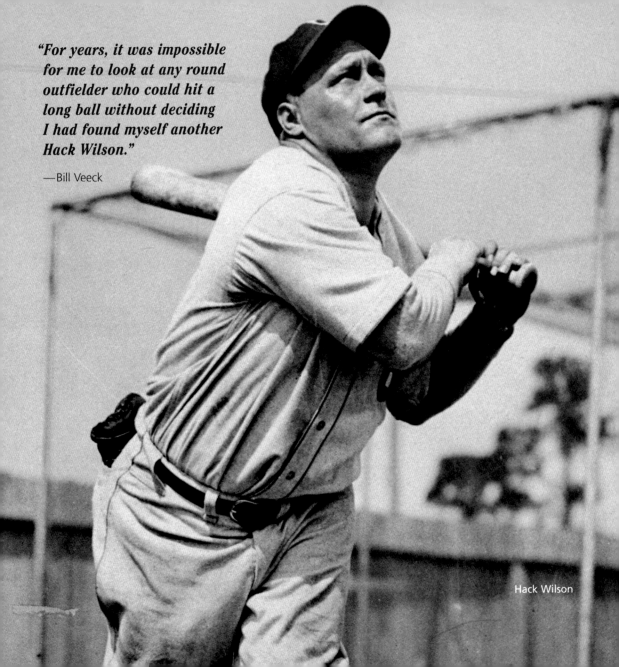

"For years, it was impossible for me to look at any round outfielder who could hit a long ball without deciding I had found myself another Hack Wilson."

—Bill Veeck

Hack Wilson

36 Hack Wilson

Lewis Robert "Hack" Wilson's 1930 season is the stuff of legends. In that year, Wilson slugged 56 home runs, an NL record for 68 years; drove in 191 runs, a major-league record that may never be broken; and batted .356. Built like a fireplug, the 5'6" Wilson was dubbed "the hardest hitting hydrant in the league." In only six seasons with the Cubs, Wilson clubbed 190 homers while batting .322. He was inducted into the Hall of Fame in 1979.

37 What I Did for Love

On July 6, 1932, the Cubs' handsome shortstop, Billy Jurges, was confronted in his hotel room by his gun-wielding girlfriend Violet Valli. Valli was distraught and insisted that Jurges promise to marry her, or she was going to kill herself. Jurges attempted to disarm her and was shot in the hand and side. He recovered and played in three of four World Series games that year, batting .364. Valli, a showgirl, signed a 22-week contract to perform in local theaters. Like a character out of the musical *Chicago*, she was billed as Violet "What I Did for Love" Valli.

Billy Jurges

Gabby Hartnett and Charlie Root

38 Charlie Root

The hard-throwing Root is the Cubs' all-time leader in wins and innings pitched. In 16 seasons with the Cubs, he won 201 games and pitched over 3,000 innings. Known as "Chinski" for throwing inside to hitters who crowded the plate, Root anchored the Cubs pitching staff in the pennant-winning seasons of 1929 and '32. He was also the pitcher of record for the Cubs when Babe Ruth supposedly called his shot in the 1932 World Series.

39 Ruth's "Called Shot"

Some say he did. Some say he didn't. The Babe never said for sure either way. But according to the legend, on October 1, 1932, as the great Babe Ruth and Cubs pitcher Charlie Root faced each other with the score tied 4–4 in the fifth inning of the third game of the World Series, Ruth gestured in the direction of Root. Many believe that Ruth was calling his shot, pointing to the bleachers in center field—where he deposited the next pitch for a home run, leading the Yankees to victory and a four-game sweep of the Cubs.

"I'd pay half my salary if I could bat in this dump all the time."

—Babe Ruth, prior to playing at Wrigley Field in the 1932 World Series

40 P.K. Wrigley

Son of William Wrigley Jr., Philip Knight Wrigley took over the Cubs when his father died in 1932. P.K. was dedicated to providing fans with a pleasant experience at the ballpark—as long as that experience didn't include high expectations for the team or night games. Plans to install lights at Wrigley Field in the early 1940s were scrapped when World War II broke out, and P.K. remained committed to day games at Wrigley for the rest of his life. He continued the tradition of Ladies Day, started by his father, and presided over the renovations of Wrigley Field in 1937–38 that brought the towering scoreboard in center field and the ivy-covered outfield walls that still define the park today. He was also the genius behind the infamous "College of Coaches" in the 1960s, when the Cubs used a rotating roster of coaches to manage the team. A private man, who spoke to newspaper reporters but didn't give radio or TV interviews, P.K. Wrigley presided over the Cubs until his death in 1977.

41 The Evil Eye

Back in the 1930s, P.K. Wrigley hired a man who claimed to be able to put a hex on opposing hitters by using his "evil eye." The wizard(?) was paid $5,000 to sit behind home plate and cast his spells. The man's powers apparently didn't extend to the weather, however. On cold days he would leave his post behind home plate and attempt to work his black magic using the ticker-tape machine in Wrigley's office upstairs. The man must have used up most of his magic conjuring the $5,000 out of Wrigley's pocket, because he was gone after a year.

"*Baseball is too much of a sport to be called a business, and too much of a business to be called a sport.*"

—Philip Wrigley

The Wrigley Building, Chicago

42 Phil Cavaretta

As an 18-year-old, Cavaretta became the everyday first baseman for the Cubs in 1935 and spent 20 consecutive seasons with the team. He quickly became a fan favorite with his competitive play and unflagging effort. He hit .355 with a career-high 97 RBI in 1945, winning the National League MVP award as he led the Cubs to their last pennant and World Series appearance. An All-Star for four consecutive years, from 1944 to 1947, Cavaretta also managed the Cubs for a brief stint in the early '50s.

43 Going Postal

The notorious bank robber John Dillinger, who became something of a folk hero during the early 1930s, is said to have attended Cubs games wearing a postal worker's uniform as a disguise.

44 Gaga for Goo Goo

In 1935, Augie "Goo Goo" Galan set a major-league record by recording 646 at bats without ever hitting into a double play. He did, however, hit into a triple play.

"Cavaretta was a hustler and the darling of the fans because he always tried to give 110 percent."

—Derek Gentile, from *The Complete Chicago Cubs*

Phil Cavaretta

45 Stan Hack

Nicknamed "Smiling Stan" by sportswriters, Hack was a popular player with his teammates and the fans. Brought to Chicago in 1932 by Bill Veeck Sr., who went to Sacramento personally to sign him to a contract, Hack became a fixture at third base. His career .301 average in 16 years with the Cubs ranks him in the top 20 all-time. A line-drive hitter who could hit to all fields, Hack performed exceptionally well in the World Series. In the '38 Series he batted .471, leading all hitters, and he batted .367 in the '45 Series, with 11 hits.

46 Billy Herman

One of the best second basemen in baseball in the 1930s and '40s, Herman hit over .300 seven times, and he led the National League in putouts six times with the Cubs. Brought in to replace the aging Rogers Hornsby, Herman batted .309 and had a .966 fielding percentage in his 11 years with the team. Leo Durocher claimed Herman was the best that he had ever seen at the hit-and-run play. He was inducted into the Hall of Fame in 1975.

Rip Collins, Billy Herman, Bill Jurges, and Stan Hack

"He was a wonderful fielder and as great a hit-and-run batter as I have ever seen."

—Charlie Grimm on Billy Herman

47 The Veecks

William Veeck Sr. was a Chicago sportswriter who was covering the baseball beat when he got a call from William Wrigley Sr. requesting his help in running the team Wrigley had recently purchased. Apparently, Veeck's harsh critiques of the club caught Wrigley's eye.

Together they made the Cubs hugely popular throughout the Midwest, by using innovative promotions and radio broadcasts to attract new fans. Veeck was instrumental in bringing in Joe McCarthy to manage the club in 1926, and he also signed Hack Wilson, Kiki Cuyler, Gabby Hartnett, and Rogers Hornsby. Veeck died in 1933, but the team he helped construct won four pennants between 1929 and 1938.

After his father died, Bill Veeck Jr. worked with P.K. Wrigley to continually improve Wrigley Field and the fans' experience. Together, they managed the renovations that brought the existing outfield bleachers, center-field scoreboard, and ivy-covered walls to the friendly confines. Always the maverick, Veeck Jr. went on to own three major-league teams and was inducted into the Hall of Fame in 1991.

48 Lights Out

The Cubs had plans to install lights in Wrigley Field late in 1941. The lights had been ordered and the steel was ready and waiting. But the attack on Pearl Harbor changed everything. P.K. Wrigley canceled the order for the lights and donated the steel to the United States war effort. There would be 47 more years of day games before lights would finally be installed at Wrigley Field.

Bill Veeck Jr.

49 The Ivy

The ivy-covered outfield walls of Wrigley Field are the defining feature of the ballpark, much the same way the Green Monster is the signature feature of Fenway Park in Boston. Owner P.K. Wrigley and general manager Bill Veeck Jr. installed the vines in 1937 as part of a major renovation that also included a new scoreboard and bleachers to expand the park's seating capacity.

To give the ballpark a more parklike feel, Wrigley and Veeck planted hundreds of ivy and bittersweet plants. Eventually the ivy took over, and today it covers the outfield's brick walls. The natural beauty the ivy brings to the park is unmatched.

Outfielders must be conscious of the fact that the lush greenery offers little or no padding, and they must learn to anticipate the irregular bounces often caused by the vines. Not all balls hit into the ivy bounce back out. Many are swallowed by the vines, prompting some players to take radical measures. Jose Cardenal is said to have hidden spare balls in the ivy in the 1970s, and Hank Sauer, "the Mayor of Wrigley Field," took advantage of the vines by stashing spare packs of chewing tobacco there that the fans had tossed to him from the bleachers.

Since it can be difficult, if not impossible, to find a ball that disappears into the ivy, anything hit there becomes a ground-rule double.

"…*the ivy on the walls, the people on the rooftops, the bleacher bums, the old stadium… it's everything you ever dreamed baseball could be.*"

—Randy Hundley

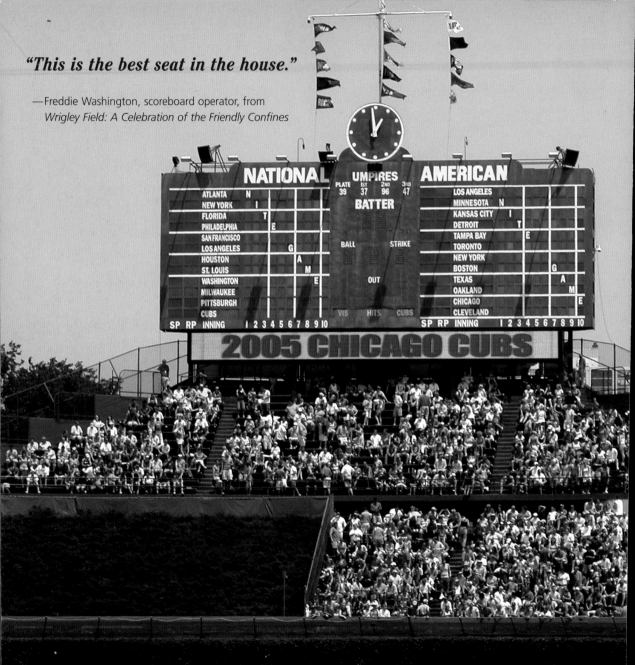

"This is the best seat in the house."

—Freddie Washington, scoreboard operator, from
Wrigley Field: A Celebration of the Friendly Confines

50 The Scoreboard

Towering above the bleachers in center field, the massive steel scoreboard was part of the 1937–38 renovations made by owner P.K. Wrigley and Bill Veeck Jr. Despite its size, the scoreboard has never been hit by a ball in play during a Cubs game. The Cubs' Bill Nicholson and Pirates great Roberto Clemente came close, but even Slammin Sammy Sosa never hit it with one of his mammoth blasts.

Although it does feature a small electronic message board at its base, most of the scoreboard is still manually operated. A staff of three to five climbs inside the giant metal box before games, peering through holes in the visitors' line score to keep track of the game. Hoisting five-pound metal plates into place to show runs, hits, and errors for the game below, they also monitor a ticker-tape machine to keep track of out-of-town scores that are updated throughout the game.

51 W for Win, L for Loss

After every game, a scoreboard crew member raises a flag announcing the game's result up a pole perched atop the scoreboard. If the Cubs have won, a white flag with a large blue W is raised. If the Cubs have lost, the flag is blue with a white L.

Every day, flags of each team are also raised in the order of the standings of the National League's three divisions. Every once in a while, the Cubs flag appears at the top.

52 Gabby Hartnett

Charles Leo "Gabby" Hartnett is probably best remembered for his "Homer in the Gloamin'" in 1938, but his solid, consistent play throughout his career earned him a spot in the Hall of Fame. Hartnett was one of the game's best catchers, leading the league in fielding percentage seven times. He was the first catcher in major-league history to top 30 home runs, 100 RBI, and a .300 batting average in a season; his numbers for the 1930 season were 37 HR, 122 RBI, and a .339 batting average. Hartnett had another great year in 1935, when he hit .344 with 13 homers and 91 RBI, winning the league MVP award, and leading the Cubs to the National League pennant.

53 The "Homer in the Gloamin'"

With darkness descending on Wrigley Field and the game tied at 5, umpires ruled that because of the fading light, no extra innings would be played. The Cubs were on the verge of taking first place from the Pirates, whose seven-game lead early in September had dwindled to just a half game as the two teams met on September 28, 1938. In the top of the ninth, the Cubs kept the Pirates off the scoreboard, but Pittsburgh hurler Mace Brown answered by retiring the first two Cubs hitters in the bottom of the inning. Up came Gabby Hartnett, the Cubs' last hope. After Brown threw two quick strikes by him, Hartnett swung mightily at the next offering and connected. The ball sailed deep into the darkening sky, over the wall, and into the bleachers for a dramatic game-winning home run, which set off one of the biggest celebrations in Wrigley Field history. The Cubs swept the three-game series against the Pirates and went on to win the NL pennant and the chance to face the Yankees in the World Series.

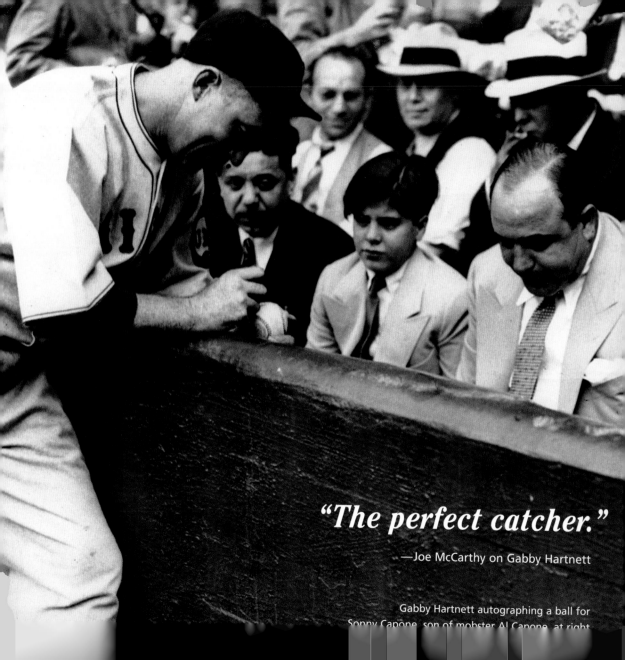

> ## "The perfect catcher."
>
> —Joe McCarthy on Gabby Hartnett

Gabby Hartnett autographing a ball for
Sonny Capone, son of mobster Al Capone, at right.

54 The Big Swish

On July 23, 1944, New York Giants manager Mel Ott elected to intentionally walk Bill Nicholson even though the bases were loaded. Nicholson, nicknamed "Swish" for the sound of his powerful swing, had already tagged Giants pitchers for four consecutive homers in the doubleheader. The move proved wise, as the Giants went on to win the game, 12–10. Swish piled up 205 home runs and 833 RBI during his 10 years with the Cubs. In 1944, the Cardinals' Marty Marion edged Nicholson for the league MVP award by a single vote.

55 Attention, Attention Please

Pat Pieper was the public-address announcer for the Cubs from 1916 through 1974. In the early days, before loudspeakers were installed, Pieper, who sat next to the backstop on a folding chair, would announce batters using a 14-pound megaphone that was just about as big as he was. Before Cubs management installed a wire basket at the top of the outfield wall, Pieper used to ask fans to "please remove their clothes." This was, of course, clothing that fans had hung over the wall, not clothing that was being worn at the time.

56 Jack Brickhouse and WGN

When WGN-TV first broadcast Cubs games in 1948, Jack Brickhouse was on the mike. It stayed that way until 1981, as Brickhouse spent more than 30 years in the Cubs' broadcast booth. Known for his bright, positive disposition and unflagging optimism, Brickhouse never seemed to be at a loss for words. His producer Arne Harris said of Brickhouse, "He was the only guy I ever met who didn't mind rain delays." Brickhouse's signature phrase, "Hey, hey," hangs from both Wrigley Field foul poles.

WGN pioneered telecasts of baseball games and, with the Cubs heading its lineup, became the nation's first TV "superstation," as cable expanded its reach throughout the Midwest, and eventually the entire United States.

"I regard sports first and foremost as entertainment... I like the 'let's forget our troubles and have some excitement' approach."

—Jack Brickhouse

57 Da Bears

The Chicago Bears also called Wrigley Field home for five decades, winning eight titles along the way. National Football League greats Gayle Sayers, Dick Butkus, Red Grange, and Bronko Nagurski are just a few of the men who fought brutal, often frigid battles on the Wrigley turf.

> *"Any team can have a bad century."*
>
> —Jack Brickhouse

58 Harry Caray

Former Cardinals and White Sox broadcaster Harry Caray replaced the legendary Jack Brickhouse in the booth in 1982 and, over time, became a legend himself. The man who pioneered the singing of "Take Me Out to the Ball Game" during the seventh-inning stretch was outspoken, opinionated, and sometimes controversial, but fans loved him. Known around Chicago as "the Mayor of Rush Street," the ever-friendly Caray was very popular with those who staffed the local bars and restaurants he frequented. His style may have been somewhat unorthodox, but he connected with the fans. After his death in 1998, the Cubs installed a statue of Caray outside the park, at the corner of Addison Street and Sheffield Avenue. A flag with his profile flies in Wrigley, ensuring that his legend will live on in Chicago.

59 Take Me Out to the Ball Game

The seventh-inning-stretch tradition created by Harry Caray is so popular that fans stay to sing even when the game's a complete blowout. Celebrities often lead the sing-along, even though many of them can't come close to carrying a tune—take Mike Ditka, for example.

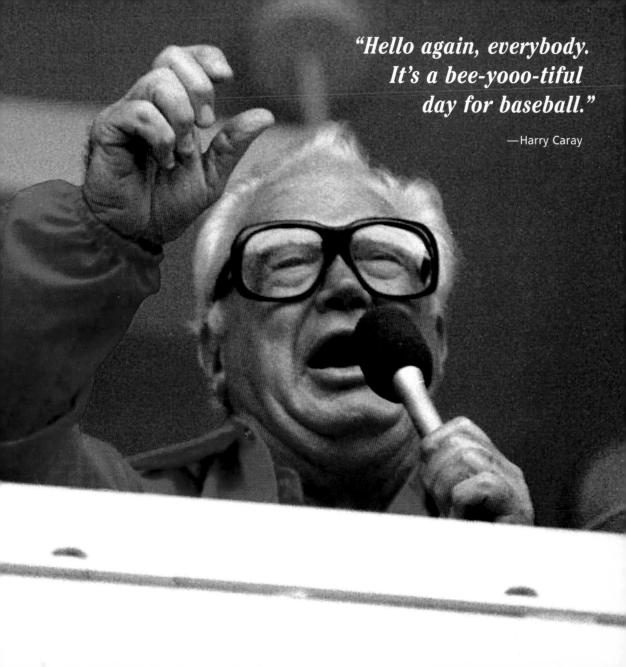

"Hello again, everybody. It's a bee-yooo-tiful day for baseball."

—Harry Caray

Andy Pafko with Ralph Kiner

60 Manning the Booth

Bob Elson and Milo Hamilton are former Cubs broadcasters who, along with Cubs legends Harry Caray and Jack Brickhouse, have been honored by the Baseball Hall of Fame. Many say Jack Quinlan was headed there too before an auto accident ended his life. In the 1930s, a young man by the name of Ronald Reagan broadcast Cubs games for WHO in Des Moines, getting his play-by-play from ticker tape wire reports. Reagan was in California covering spring training when he visited Hollywood and sat for his first screen test. That prompted him to leave radio for the movies, where he became a big star. Eventually he found his way into politics.

Ronald Reagan

61 Andy Pafko

Dubbed "Handy Andy" by manager Charlie Grimm for his versatility, Pafko was a four-time All-Star for the Cubs with his brilliant play in center field and at third base. He led the league in fielding percentage in 1945, with a .995 mark, and batted over .300 four times while he was with the Cubs. Traded to the Brooklyn Dodgers in 1951, Pafko was playing left field when the Giants' Bobby Thomson hit the homer that became known as the "Shot Heard 'Round the World."

62 1945

P.K. Wrigley fired manager Jimmie Wilson after the 1944 season and brought back "Jolly Cholly" Grimm as skipper for 1945. The Cubs fielded a solid team, which featured Stan Hack, Andy Pafko, Swish Nicholson, and Phil Cavaretta, who would win the National League MVP award that year. The key to the year, however, was Chicago's late-season acquisition of pitcher Hank Borowy off waivers from the Yankees. Borowy went 11–2 for the Cubs, with a sterling 2.13 ERA, as Chicago edged the Musial–less Cardinals for the pennant. Facing the Detroit Tigers again in the World Series, the Cubs took a 2-games-to-1 lead behind the pitching of Borowy and Claude Passeau, who threw a one-hitter in Game 3. With all the remaining games to be played in Chicago, the Cubs were in perfect position to seize their first championship since 1908. But the Tigers won the first two games at Wrigley, to lead 3 games to 2, and put the Cubs on the brink of another Series failure. In Game 6, Stan Hack was the hero, driving in the winning run with a twelfth-inning double, as Borowy recorded the win with four innings of relief. In the deciding game, Grimm opted to start Borowy, despite his work in Game 6—the Tigers pounced, scoring five runs in the first and cruising to a 9–3 win. That was the last time a World Series game was played at Wrigley Field.

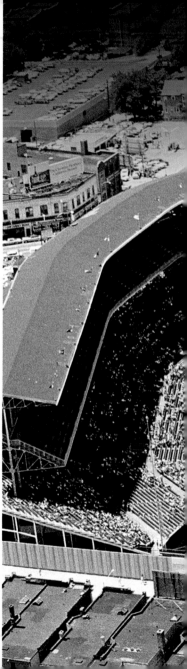

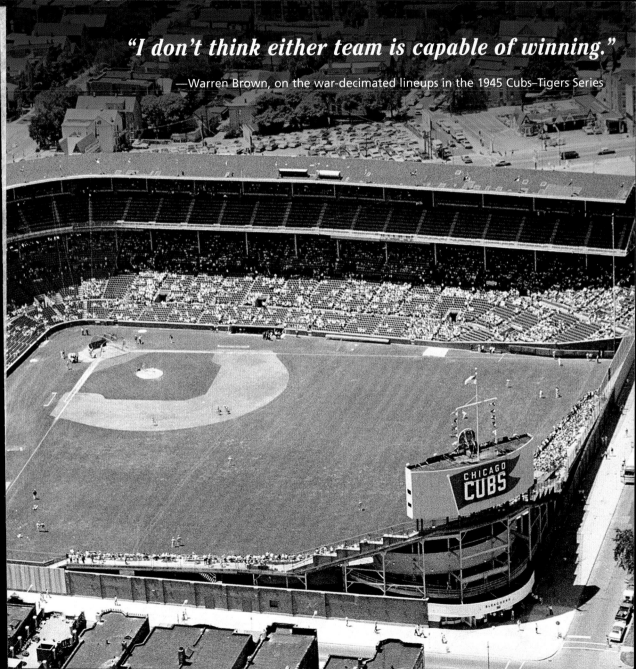

"I don't think either team is capable of winning."

—Warren Brown, on the war-decimated lineups in the 1945 Cubs–Tigers Series

Sam Sianis, owner of the
Billy Goat Tavern in Chicago

63 Curses

In 1945, local tavern owner William Sianis, for reasons that aren't really clear, brought his pet goat to Wrigley Field for a game. Concerned about the goat's smell, among other things, ushers turned away Sianis and his pet, even though he had a ticket for the horned beast. Outraged, Sianis put a curse on the Cubs—and they went on to lose the World Series to the Tigers in seven games. The Cubs haven't been to the Series since. Over time, the story has become known as the "Curse of the Billy Goat."

Although the theory isn't nearly as popular as the "Curse of the Billy Goat," some speculate that the reason for the Cubs' litany of failure over the years comes from the Man Upstairs. Their rationale? Wrigley Field was built on the grounds of a former seminary, and the Big Man isn't happy about it. It's something to think about, given that the Cubs haven't won a World Series in all the years they've been playing there.

64 The Mad Russian

Lou Novikoff, a four-time minor-league batting champion nicknamed "the Mad Russian," unfortunately didn't enjoy the same level of success in the majors. But he did earn his own place in Cubs history when he stole third base . . . with the bases loaded. When asked why he did it, he answered, "I got such a good jump on the pitcher, I couldn't resist."

65 The Rifleman

Chuck Connors, who went on to fame as the star of the TV show *The Rifleman*, played 66 games at first base for the Cubs in 1951, batting .239 with two home runs. Guess his aim with a rifle was a little better than with a bat.

66 The Lovable Losers

In 1948, the Cubs became the first last-place team to draw 1 million fans, and over time the team became known as "the Lovable Losers." Still, most fans seem to take the moniker in stride, and they don't seem to be haunted by past failures like fans from a prominent East Coast American League team. For the most part, Cubs fans accept their fate and will tell you they have no desire to be the subject of a John Updike or Stephen King essay on their tragic existence. Heck, they even like Bill Buckner, who spent seven-plus seasons with the Cubs. So they haven't won a World Series since 1908! They'll get one eventually.

67 Number 96

Bill Voiselle spent the last year, 1950, of his nine-year major-league career with the Cubs. The right-handed pitcher, who once won 21 games for the New York Giants, wore the number 96, the highest number ever worn by a Cub. His hometown? Ninety-six, South Carolina.

68 Hank Sauer

Known as "the Mayor of Wrigley Field," Sauer was extremely popular with Cubs fans. In 1952, at the age of 35, he won the National League MVP award, belting 37 home runs and knocking in a league-leading 121 runs. A big, tobacco-chewing outfielder, Sauer's adoring fans used to toss him packs of chew, which he crammed in his pockets. What he couldn't carry he would stash in the ivy growing on the outfield wall.

"I lost the ball
in the moon."

—Hank Sauer

"Let's play two."

—Ernie Banks

69 Ernie Banks

The early May day was cold and miserable, with rain limiting attendance to 5,000-plus fans. The Atlanta Braves' Pat Jarvis was on the mound. Thirty-nine-year-old Ernie Banks stepped to the plate in the second inning and launched a long drive to left. Back went Braves left fielder Rico Carty, to the track. But the ball sailed over the fence and into the bleachers, then caromed back onto the field. Banks rounded the bases for the 500th time, becoming the first Cub to hit 500 home runs.

The man known to everyone as "Mr. Cub" played 2,528 games for the club without ever making a postseason appearance. Despite that, Banks loved playing in Chicago, and he would often remind everyone by reciting his signature phrase, "Let's play two." When he joined the team in 1953, he became the first black player to appear in a game for the Cubs, and Banks' sunny disposition and excellence on the field quickly won over the fans.

He won the league MVP award in 1958 and 1959, with 47 and 45 home runs, respectively. For his career, Banks hit 512 home runs with 1,636 RBI, second all-time for the Cubs in both categories. In 1977, Banks was inducted into the Hall of Fame, and his number 14 was the first number to be retired by the Cubs.

CUBS

ERNIE BANKS   1st base

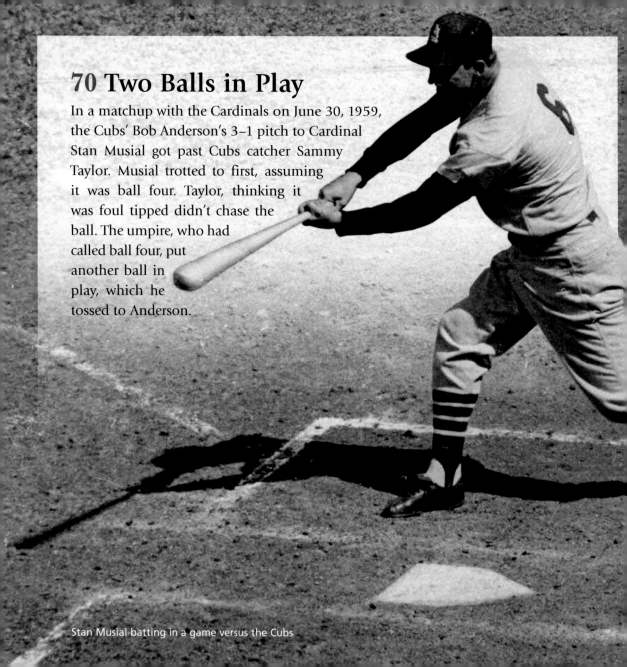

70 Two Balls in Play

In a matchup with the Cardinals on June 30, 1959, the Cubs' Bob Anderson's 3–1 pitch to Cardinal Stan Musial got past Cubs catcher Sammy Taylor. Musial trotted to first, assuming it was ball four. Taylor, thinking it was foul tipped didn't chase the ball. The umpire, who had called ball four, put another ball in play, which he tossed to Anderson.

Stan Musial batting in a game versus the Cubs

While this was taking place, the ballboy grabbed the original ball and handed it to the public-address announcer, Pat Pieper, who sat by the backstop and supplied the umpire with new balls. Cubs third baseman Alvin Dark, thinking it was a live ball, grabbed it from Pieper and threw it to Ernie Banks, who was covering second base as Musial sensed the confusion and headed for the bag. At the same time, Anderson saw Musial on his way to second and fired his ball to Banks too. Anderson's throw sailed into center field as Banks caught Dark's throw and tagged Musial, who'd come off the bag. Musial ignored the tag with ball one and headed for third. Cubs center fielder Bobby Thomson gathered up Anderson's ball and fired it past third and into the Cubs' dugout. Eventually the umpires sorted out the mess, calling Musial out at second. The Cardinals protested, but won the game 4-1, anyway.

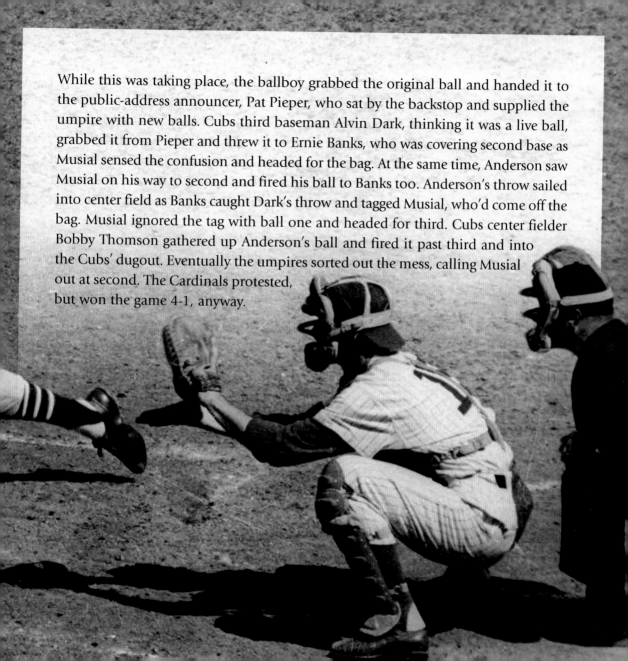

Don Cardwell is mobbed by fans
after pitching a no-hitter

71 The Golden Toothpick

After walking the bases loaded in the ninth inning of the May 12, 1955, Cubs–Pirates game, Sam "Toothpick" Jones of the Cubs struck out the last three batters to preserve his no-hitter, a 4–0 win. It was the first no-hitter by a black pitcher in major-league history, and the first no-hitter in Wrigley Field since the double no-hitter of 1917. Before the game, TV announcer Harry Creighton joked with the toothpick-chewing Jones that he'd give Jones a gold toothpick if the pitcher threw a no-hitter. Creighton kept his word.

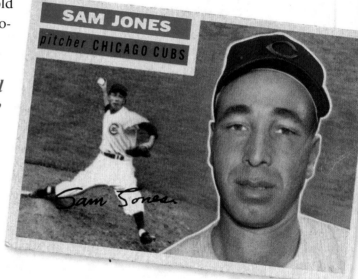

SAM JONES

pitcher CHICAGO CUBS

"You've never seen a curveball until you've seen Sam Jones' curveball. If you were a right-handed hitter that ball was a good four feet behind you."

—Hobie Landrith

72 The New Guy

On May 15, 1960, just two days after being traded from the Phillies, Don Cardwell no-hit the Cardinals 4–0 in his first start for the Cubs. Ernie Banks homered and right fielder George Altman made a spectacular eighth-inning grab of Carl Sawatski's drive to preserve the gem. It was the first time the Cards had been no-hit since May 11, 1919.

73 Billy Williams

Soft-spoken Williams was the best left-handed hitter in Cubs history—incredibly consistent and dependable. From 1960 through 1974, his last year with the Cubs, Williams never hit lower than .276, and he belted 20 or more home runs in 13 consecutive seasons, including a career-high 42 in 1970. His 1,117 consecutive games played was a National League record until Steve Garvey broke it in 1983. Williams' number 26 was retired by the Cubs in 1987 and hangs on the right-field foul pole in Wrigley Field. He was inducted into the Hall of Fame in 1987.

BILLY WILLIAMS
CHICAGO CUBS
OF

74 10, 14, 23, and 26

High atop the left-field foul pole are flags that sport Cubs greats Ron Santo's number 10 and Ernie Banks' number 14. Flying from the right-field foul pole are Billy Williams' number 26 and Ryne Sandberg's number 23.

Pennants commemorating other Cubs greats and their achievements fly high above the field along the edge of the rooftop above the upper deck.

"*Billy Williams is the best hitter, day in and day out, I have ever seen.... He didn't hit for just one or two days, or one or two weeks. He hit all the time.*"

—Don Kessinger

"I made a game effort to argue but two things were against me: the umpires and the rules."

—Leo Durocher

75 The College of Coaches

In the early 1960s, owner P.K. Wrigley, frustrated at his managers' lack of success with the Cubs, decided to put together a "College of Coaches." There was no manager. Instead, a roster of coaches rotated through the minor-league system and up to the Cubs every few weeks. This headless system failed miserably, as the Cubs finished 29 games out of first place in 1961, and a staggering 42 1/2 games out in '62. It was an idea way ahead of its time—if it ever had a time—but then again, what did the Cubs have to lose?

76 Leo Durocher

After five miserable years that began with the "College of Coaches" experiment, P.K. Wrigley hired Leo Durocher to manage the Cubs in 1966. Leo the Lip was known as a combative, tough-as-nails, win-at-all-costs manager who could build a winning team, and that's just what Chicago needed. He insisted that Wrigley open his wallet and spend more money on quality players. Durocher's first season was no better than the previous years, as the Cubs lost 103 games. But Durocher gradually brought in the talent he needed to field a winner, trading for Fergie Jenkins and Randy Hundley, to team with Banks, Williams, Ron Santo, and emerging stars Glenn Beckert and Don Kessinger. The Cubs finished in third place in 1967 and '68. Then, in 1969, the Cubs began the season 11–1, and they led the surprising Mets by 7 1/2 games in late August. But the "Amazin' Mets" swept by the stumbling Cubs in September to win the division, while the Cubs finished second. Durocher's Cubs finished second again in 1970, and he was let go in 1972. Although he never brought a pennant to Chicago, Durocher instilled a winning attitude and did bring respectability back to the franchise.

77 1969

The Cubs led the National League East Division for 155 straight days before stumbling near the finish line and finishing second to the "Amazin' Mets." It's the longest period any team has ever held first place without winning the pennant.

78 The Bleacher Bums

Seating is unreserved in Wrigley's outfield bleachers, and the atmosphere is often the same. Given the right combination of weather, baseball, and liquid refreshment, the bleachers can become one big party. Bare chests and bikini tops are common sights on warm, sunny days.

It's here that the Bleacher Bums can be found. The original group got its name back in the 1960s after a couple of the regulars brought in a sign made from a bedsheet with a hole in it. One of the "bums" would stick his or her head through the hole in the sign, which read "Hit the Bleacher Bum."

79 Throw It Back

It's never a good thing when an opponent launches a long ball into the great beyond for a home run. At Wrigley, Cubs fans have made it a tradition to graciously return these not-so-special deliveries by tossing the balls back onto the field after they arrive unsolicited in the bleachers.

80 Murphy's Bleachers

At the corner of Waveland and Sheffield avenues is a little place known as Murphy's Bleachers. Formerly Ernie's Bleachers, then JB's Bleachers and Ray's Bleachers, Murphy's is a popular spot that offers much-needed liquid refreshment to fans—one of at least a dozen bustling local taverns near Wrigley Field. And, if the walk across the street to Wrigley is just too much to ask after a little pre-game libation, fans can even stay and watch the game there.

81 Ronnie "Woo Woo"

Cubs, Woo! Cubs, Woo! If Ronnie "Woo Woo" Wickers is anywhere nearby, his piercing chant will find your ears at most Cubs games. The uniform-clad Wickers makes his presence known in the neighborhoods around the park, and to the fans who sit anywhere near him out in the bleachers, as he cheers for his beloved Cubs. His shriek may be annoying to fans looking for a more serene experience, but to most, Woo Woo has become an unofficial mascot. His popularity led local filmmaker Paul Hoffman to direct and produce a documentary on Wickers, titled *WooLife*.

82 Almost Perfect

Despite suffering from a bad cold and a sore elbow, Cubs pitcher Milt Pappas retired the first 26 San Diego Padres batters he faced on September 2, 1972. With a 1–2 count on Padres pinch-hitter Larry Stahl, Pappas threw three straight balls, walking Stahl and ending his bid for a perfect game. Pappas did retire the next batter, however, to preserve his no-hitter. It was the Cubs' second no-hitter of the season; rookie Burt Hooten had tossed a "no-no" of his own on April 16.

83 Ron Santo

If Ernie Banks wasn't already known as Mr. Cub, Ron Santo might be. The standout third baseman was a Cubs leader for 14 years, smacking 20 or more home runs in 11 of those seasons and eclipsing 100 RBI in a season four times. His 337 home runs is fourth all-time for Chicago. Despite the Cubs' lack of success, Santo won five consecutive Gold Gloves and was a nine-time All-Star.

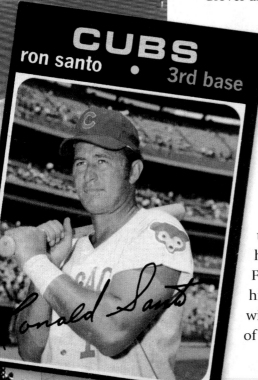

On July 6, 1970, Santo had a career day. In the first game of a doubleheader versus the Montreal Expos, he launched a game-winning two-run homer, and in the nightcap, Santo drove in eight runs with two more round-trippers and a bases-loaded walk. The Cubs won the games 3–2 and 14–2.

After retiring as a player, Santo joined the Cubs' broadcast team. His number 10 hangs with Ernie Banks' 14 from Wrigley Field's left-field foul pole, commemorating his achievements as a Cub. Most Cubs fans will tell you Santo should be in the Hall of Fame.

84 Fergie Jenkins

Used primarily as a relief pitcher in 1966 after joining the Cubs in a trade with the Philadelphia Phillies, Jenkins was converted to a starter in 1967 by manager Leo Durocher. The move paid big dividends as Jenkins delivered six consecutive 20-win seasons. He led the Cubs in wins, starts, complete games, innings pitched, and strikeouts during the span. In 1971, Jenkins won 24 games and the National League Cy Young award. A control pitcher who kept hitters off balance by changing speeds, Jenkins is beloved by Cubs fans. He was traded away in 1974, but returned in 1982 to finish his career as a Cub. Jenkins became the first Canadian to be inducted into the Hall of Fame, in 1991.

"Your stuff is never good unless you can throw strikes. He can. And he can throw them all day."

—Joe Becker on Fergie Jenkins

85 Monday Saves the Flag

It was April 25, 1976. A couple of would-be protesters dashed onto the Dodger Stadium field as the Dodgers were batting in the fourth inning of a game against the Cubs. They spread an American flag on the outfield grass like a picnic blanket, then doused it with lighter fluid. The Cubs' Rick Monday, who was patrolling center field, saw the two goons attempting to light a match and burn the flag. The first match died, and while they tried a second one, Monday sprinted across the field, grabbed the flag, and gave it to Dodgers pitcher Doug Rau. A month later, when the Dodgers came to Chicago, Al Campanis, a Dodgers executive, presented the flag to Monday, and it still hangs in his house today. Evidently Monday made quite an impression; the Dodgers traded for him the following year, in a five-player deal that brought Bill Buckner to the Cubs.

86 Save Me

The Cubs have had a few great closers in their time. Bruce Sutter won the Cy Young award in 1979, with 37 saves and an ERA of 2.22. Lee Smith totaled 180 saves in eight seasons with the Cubs, recording more than 30 saves in each year from 1984 to 1987. And Randy Myers saved a team-record 53 games in 1993.

87 Mad Dog

Bill "Mad Dog" Madlock won back-to-back batting titles in 1975 (.354) and 1976 (.339), the only Cub ever to do so. Madlock's 1976 title was particularly impressive, as he went 4-for-4 on the final day of the season to raise his average by six points, just edging out Ken Griffey Sr. Madlock holds the highest career batting average of any Cub player, at .336.

Rick Monday is honored by the VFW

"Nobody made playing second base look easier than Ryne Sandberg."

—Ron Santo in *Few and Chosen*

88 Ryne Sandberg

In what became one of the best trades ever for the Cubs, Sandberg came to Chicago in 1982 as part of a deal that sent Ivan DeJesus to Philadelphia for Larry Bowa. After a year at third base, the Cubs switched Ryno to second base, where he became one of the best ever to play the game, winning nine consecutive Gold Gloves. A terrific hitter as well, Sandberg batted better than .300 five times and smashed 25 or more home runs six times, including 40 in 1990. In 1984, he was named National League MVP, leading the Cubs to the postseason for the first time since 1945.

On June 23, 1984, with the St. Louis Cardinals in town, Ryno had a day to remember. The Cards jumped all over the Cubs, taking a 7–0 lead. But the Cubs whittled away and came to bat in the bottom of the ninth trailing by the score of 9–8. Sandberg stepped up to the plate and promptly deposited a Bruce Sutter sinker into the seats to tie the game. The Cards took an 11–9 lead in the top of the tenth, but with one on in the bottom of the inning, Sandberg took Sutter deep once more to tie the game for a second time. The Cubs went on to win in the eleventh, and it became forever known as "the Sandberg Game." For the day, Sandberg was 5-for-6 with seven RBI. Sandberg's number 23 was retired by the Cubs in 2005, a few weeks after he was elected to the Hall of Fame.

89 A Dying Cub Fan's Last Request

Acclaimed singer-songwriter Steve Goodman wrote the timeless classic "A Dying Cub Fan's Last Request" as an ode to his star-crossed team. The song debuted on Roy Leonard's WGN radio show in 1983, and can still be heard regularly each spring as baseball season begins. Goodman also wrote the 1984 Cubs' theme, "Go Cubs Go."

90 1984

In 1984, the Cubs reached the postseason for the first time since 1945 by winning the National League East pennant. The team was solid, with talent at every position. Young phenom Ryne Sandberg was coming into his own at second base, and Rick Sutcliffe, a mid-season addition to the pitching staff, had provided an unbelievable boost by going 16–1 from June through the end of September. After winning the first two games of the NLCS 13–0 and 4–2 over the San Diego Padres, it looked as if the Cubs were at last on their way to the World Series again. But lest we forget, this is the Cubs we're talking about. The Padres responded with two straight victories to even the series. The Cubs quickly took control of the deciding game, jumping out to a 3–0 lead after two innings, but with the score 3–2 in the seventh, the Padres put another dagger into the Cubs' heart, scoring four runs to win the game 6–3. It was one of the Cubs' most heartbreaking losses, in a history littered with heartbreaking losses.

*"I went to the bathroom and it was 3–0 [Cubs].
I came out and it was 6–3. I'm never going to
the bathroom again."*

—Sharon Streicher, at Murphy's Bleachers for Game 5
of the 1984 NLCS versus the Padres

Ryne Sandberg

"Maddux is a cerebral assassin on the mound. He knows his strengths and limitations as well as those of every hitter." —Stats, Inc.

Greg Maddux

91 The Human Rain Delay

Acquired from Cleveland in 1984 in a mid-season trade, Rick Sutcliffe went 16–1 for the Cubs, leading them to the National League East title, and was the first pitcher ever to win the Cy Young award after pitching in both leagues in the same year. Injuries limited his contribution the next two seasons, but he won a league-leading 18 games in 1987 and 16 more in 1989, as the Cubs returned to the playoffs. Pain from his assorted injuries became so persistent that Sutcliffe would have to step off the mound between pitches to let it subside. Because of this, players took to calling him "the Human Rain Delay."

92 The Hawk

Andre "the Hawk" Dawson signed an "open" contract with the Cubs in 1987, letting the team set the terms. He gave the Cubs a huge return on their investment when he slugged 49 home runs, along with 137 RBI and a .287 batting average, becoming the first player ever to win the league MVP award while playing for a last-place team.

93 Greg Maddux

From 1988 to 1992, Maddux won 15 or more games each season, including his 20-win, 199-strikeout season of 1992, when he won the first of his four Cy Young awards. Maddux left the Cubs for the Braves in 1993, but he returned to Chicago in 2004, much to the delight of Cubs fans. After 20 years in the majors, Maddux has become one of the best control pitchers ever, and he is one of only nine pitchers in history with 300 wins and 3,000 strikeouts.

"Someone said it's like the good Lord letting us know that he's a little sad, too."

—Rick Sutcliffe, commenting on the rainout of Wrigley Field's first night game

94 Let There Be Light

On August 8, 1988, over 40 years after lights were installed at Tiger Stadium, the next-to-last ballpark to get lights, night baseball came to Wrigley Field. Harry Grossman, a 92-year-old fan, threw the switch, and the Cubs took the field to face the Philadelphia Phillies. But, ironically, rain came and the game was washed out. The Cubs were back the next night to face the Mets. This time the rain held off, and the Cubs won the first official night game played at Wrigley, 6–4.

95 Mark Grace

Grace joined the Cubs in 1988 and promptly
served notice that he came to play, winning the
Sporting News Rookie of the Year award with a
.296 batting average and seven home runs. He
followed up his rookie campaign by hitting .314
in 1989 and .304 in '90. In his 13-year career
with the Cubs, Amazing Grace batted .308 and
his 456 doubles are second on the Cubs' all-time
list. Though not as high-profile as fellow Cubs
Ryne Sandberg, Andre Dawson, and Sammy Sosa,
Grace was a solid performer whose consistency
made him a fan favorite. He won four Gold
Gloves at first base and hit .647 in the 1989
NLCS against the Giants. His number 17 is on
one of the commemorative flags that adorn the
upper deck of Wrigley Field.

*"The music sounds better, the wine
tastes sweeter, and the girls look
better when we win."*

—Mark Grace

96 Sammy Sosa

The face of the Cubs in the late 1990s and early 21st century, Sosa hit more home runs than any other Cub, even the great Ernie Banks. Sosa came to Chicago in 1992 in a trade for George Bell, and the underachieving Sosa quickly developed into one of the most dominant power hitters the game has ever seen. In 1998, Sosa hit an incredible 20 home runs just in the month of June, and 66 for the year in a historic battle with the Cardinals' Mark McGwire. Both broke Roger Maris' single-season record of 61 that had stood since 1961. Sosa also led the league in RBI with 158. He was voted the league's MVP as the Cubs made it to the playoffs for the first time in nine years. Slammin' Sammy followed his record-breaking season with 63 more dingers in 1999 and 64 in 2001, becoming the first player ever to hit 60 or more home runs three times.

97 The Great Race

The summer of 1998 was one for the ages. The Cubs' Sammy Sosa and the Cardinals' Mark McGwire were each hitting home runs at a remarkable clip. As the season entered its final month, Sosa and McGwire were neck and neck, just a few homers shy of the all-time record. McGwire got there first, hammering number 62 on September 8 as the Cards faced the Cubs at Busch Stadium in St. Louis. Five days later, on September 13, Sosa smacked his 61st homer off Brewers hurler Bronswell Patrick in the fifth inning. To add to the drama, Sosa followed that with number 62 off Eric Plunk in the bottom of the ninth, sending the game into extra innings. The Cubs won the game, 11–10, when Mark Grace homered with Sosa on deck. For the season, McGwire hit 70 homers and Sosa finished with 66.

Kerry Wood

98 20 Ks for Kerry

In one of the most remarkable pitching performances ever, 20-year-old Cubs rookie Kerry Wood struck out 20 Houston Astros to tie the all-time major-league record set by Roger Clemens. Wood came into the May 6, 1998, start with a 2–2 record and sporting an ERA of almost 6. But on this day, he was nearly perfect, fanning the side four times and holding the Astros to just one hit. The Cubs honored Wood's performance by placing a flag with the number 20 on it on Wrigley's rooftop.

99 Derrek's Quest

From the beginning of the 2005 season, Derrek Lee was among the National League leaders in home runs, RBI, and batting average, prompting talk of a possible Triple Crown. As July turned to August, he led the league in homers and batting average and was third in RBI. With a 2-homer day on August 28, Lee set a Cubs record for home runs in a season by a first baseman, with his 38th and 39th. He fell short of winning the Triple Crown, but Lee did win the NL batting title with a .335 average, and finshed second in home runs with 46. The last NL player to win the Triple Crown was the Cardinals' Joe Medwick, in 1937.

100 Bartman

The Cubs were five outs away from their first World Series appearance since 1945. They were leading the Florida Marlins 3 games to 2, and up 3–0 in the eighth inning of Game 6 of the 2003 NLCS, when Luis Castillo came to the plate for the Marlins. Castillo lifted a high pop down the third-base line, and as it drifted toward the seats Cubs left fielder Moises Alou gave chase. Fans in the box seats behind the bullpen rose as one for the potential souvenir. As luck would have it, the ball fell just foul, inches into the stands. As Alou jumped and reached over the wall to make the catch, fan Steve Bartman, who had been following the flight of the ball rather than Alou's movements, also reached for the souvenir and inadvertently knocked it away from Alou. The left fielder slammed his glove down in disgust. Castillo regrouped and drew a walk. Then, after Ivan Rodriguez drove in the Marlins' first run with a single, Miguel Cabrera hit what should have been an inning-ending double-play grounder to shortstop Alex Gonzalez. But Gonzalez bobbled the ball, the inning continued, and the Marlins scored seven more runs, winning the game 8–3. They went on to win Game 7 and then defeated the Yankees in the World Series.

The next day, the Bartman hunt began. Radio DJs began tracking down the mysterious fan's name and whereabouts. Several fans in Bartman's proximity were misidentified as the culprit. Then someone identified his workplace, forcing his entire company to shut down. At one point, it was rumored that Bartman would have to leave Chicago, and Governor Jeb Bush officially offered him sanctuary in Florida—further enraging Cubs fans.

"I am so truly sorry from the bottom of this Cubs fan's broken heart."

—Steve Bartman

101 Hope for the Future

Just because it's been six decades since the Cubs made it to the World Series and nearly a century since they won one doesn't mean it'll never happen. It will. Just keep believing. Always believe.

Acknowledgments

First and foremost, a special word of thanks goes out to Leslie Stoker, Jennifer Levesque, and the rest of the folks at Stewart, Tabori & Chang for their tireless support and patience with this project.

I would also like to thank my dear friend (and art director) Mary Tiegreen, who conceived this series of books, continues to astound me with her vision and creativity, and makes every day a sunny day. And her husband, Hubert, who doesn't care nearly as much about baseball as golf. His friendship gets me away from the computer and out on the course for a much-needed breath of fresh air.

To Kevin O'Sullivan at AP/Wide World, Bill Burdick at the National Baseball Hall of Fame Library, Colleen Beckett and Aimee Marshall of the Chicago Historical Society, Lewis Wyman at the Library of Congress, and Charlie Gillingham of the Chicago Cubs media department, thank you for all your time and effort.

To Bob Shaw and Floyd Sullivan, lifelong Cubs devotees, a standing ovation for all your insights, factoids, and bits of trivia that add so much to this book. Thanks for sharing your fond memories and your scars.

And, finally, to my team — my beautiful wife, Mary; amazingly talented daughter, Savannah; brilliant son, Dakota; and good pal Sam, the dog; my parents, Ron and Beth, who always provide a soft place to land; my brother Ron, who wrote the companion Cardinals book; my sister Edie, who I see all too rarely; and the rest of the Greens, McGlones, and Mathwichs — you're the best. Forever, thank you for your love and support.

A Tiegreen Book

Text copyright © 2006 David Green
Compilation copyright © 2006
Mary Tiegreen

Published in 2006 by
Stewart, Tabori & Chang
115 West 18th Street
New York, NY 10011
www.abramsbooks.com

Editor: Jennifer Levesque
Designer: David Green, Brightgreen Design
Production Manager: Kim Tyner

Library of Congress
Cataloging-in-Publication Data

Green, David, 1959-
  101 reasons to love the Cubs /
  David Green
    p. cm.
  ISBN 1-58479-499-2
  1. Chicago Cubs (Baseball team)—
    Miscellanea.
    I. Title: One hundred one reasons to
    love the Cubs. II. Title: One hundred
    and one reasons to love the Cubs.
    III. Title.

GV875.C6G74 2006
796.357'640977311--dc22
2005024646

101 Reasons to Love the Cubs is a book in the 101 REASONS TO LOVE™ series.

101 REASONS TO LOVE™ is a trademark of Mary Tiegreen and Hubert Pedroli.

Printed in China

10 9 8 7 6 5 4 3 2 1

First Printing

Stewart, Tabori & Chang is a subsidiary of

LA MARTINIÈRE
G R O U P E

Photo Credits

Pages 1, 2-3, 7, 24-25, 29, 38, 41, 48, 49 (inset), 53, 54, 56-57, 59, 65, 66, 69, 70, 72, 73 (inset), 75, 76, 79, 80, 82-83, 84, 88, 94, 96 (inset), 97, 99, 100, 103, 104, 106-107, 109, 111, 112, 113, 116-117, and 118 courtesy of AP/Wide World Photos.

Pages 17, 21, 31, 37, 44, 50, and 67 courtesy of the Chicago Historical Society.

Pages 4-5, 8 (cap), 10, 26, 32-33, 35, 61, 62, 81 (card), 85 (card), 86 (card), 87, 91, 92, and 95 (card), 119, and 120 (Brock card) courtesy of David Green, Brightgreen Design.

Pages 8-9 (background), 12, 13, 14, 18-19 (background), 19 (cards), 20, 23, 28, 42-43, 46-47 and 120 (M. Brown card) courtesy of the Library of Congress Prints and Photographs Division.

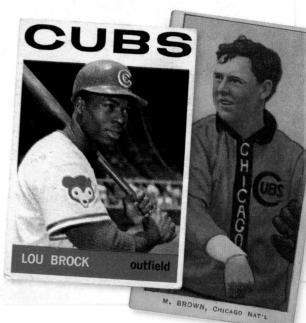